BE

Words and Poetry by
Will Espero

Published by JMFdeA Press in 2024

ISBN: 978-1-956695-20-5
Hardcover

ISBN: 978-1-956695-21-2
Paperback

ISBN: 978-1-956695-22-9
E-Book

ISBN: 978-1-956695-23-6
Audio

JMFdeA Press
P.O. Box 235737
Honolulu, HI 96823
www.jmfdeapress.com

This is my collection of poetry, prose, and
thoughts I have created over the decades of
my existence. I hope you enjoy the feelings,
messages, and images conveyed.

This book is dedicated to my dad, Victoriano Dungca Espero, who passed away on March 16, 2024. His dream and vision are why I am who I am today.

GENESIS

Liquid fire

does inspire

snaking to the ocean floor,

Glowing river

sends a shiver

as we yearn to see much more,

A breathing land with

blackened sand

acid steam will choke the sky,

Nature's law

a crowd in awe

hoping it will never die,

Pele's show

islands grow

more powerful than man will be,

Liquid fire

does inspire

as it meets the waiting sea.

PERFORMANCE

Flaming sparkles dance
as the sun casts
a golden blanket below.
A clear glassy shield
covers the sandy beach
absorbed by tiny grains,
then, formed again
by another sculpting wave.
Gulls float
falling to the earth
to feast on those
abandoned by the sea.
A breeze brings ripples
to the watery stage
as a mother whale and her babe
dive and dance in pure perfection
to the delight of a captivated sun.
Come night, the gulls will sleep
but the scene will be the same
as the moon and her stars
witness a flawless show.

BANYANS

Giant banyans stretch their limbs
Reaching for the vacant land,
Underneath the sun is dim
Rooted trunks grow and expand.

Once seedlings, small no more
Solid strength beyond compare,
Deep within the earthen floor
Smell the banyans in the air.

Aged trees have seen the past
Witnessed more than the average man,
Nature's creation destined to last
Ready for the final stand.

THE STORM

Legions of rain invaded our land

Soaking the earth, nourishing man.

Flooding waters seeking a path

Nature boasting its mighty wrath.

Forests and grassland feeling the drench

Empty rivers suddenly quenched.

Looming clouds guard the sky

Winds surround the menacing eye.

THE STREAM

The twisting stream trickles
under fallen rotting branches
near smoothed stones
half buried by powdered silt.

Shaded canopies of green
filter precious sunlight
as the mountain rain
lazily flows to the sea.

Stealth crayfish
capture resting minnows
as cautious birds hop
along the bank
to quench an afternoon thirst.

Skinny roots exposed
by the constant surge
provide a haven for
hungry mosquitoes
waiting for naked legs.

CRABS

Statute crabs
resting on lava
silently scan the beach,

As children approach
the crabs slowly move
to avoid the red net's reach,

The ocean's drizzle
thrown towards the shore
sends the crabs on a scurry,

A rolling swell
slams into the rocks
inviting a liquid fury,

The clinging crabs
disappear in the foam
seeking a place to hide,

Another swell forms
meeting the isle
attracting the rising tide.

CANE FIRE

Watching from the mountain
in the darkness of morning
a broken lei of fire
swarms the Ewa Plain.
Rested field hands
divert the blazing wall
as tall green stalks
succumb to a heated harvest.
The smell of smoke
follows the wind
and crisp blackened cane
fall to swinging machetes.
Drifting gray ash
like weightless snowflakes
invade neighboring homes.
The truck load is hauled away
as another fertile field
will soon crackle from the torch.

THE EWA PLAIN

Long ago on the Ewa Plain
In the west with little rain
Grew thousands of acres of sugar cane
Dillingham had his locomotive train

Long ago on the Ewa Plain
White men came to profit and gain
Laborers worked and felt the pain
The burning harvests left their stain

Long ago on the Ewa Plain
Rivers and streams would feel the drain
The aina absorbed the precious rain
Immigrants felt the human strain

Now today on the Ewa Plain
We have a historical tourist train
Fields are empty of sugar cane
But it's still very hot with little rain

Yes, today on the Ewa Plain
Families grow and students gain
A new city grows to help the strain
Plantation history will always remain

SERENITY OF NIGHT

The sun sets on these glorious isles
Seabirds flock to waiting nests,
As a quiet breeze goes by
Darkness emerges east to west.

Serenity of night captures my mind
Soothing visions of restless waves,
A cry of passion pierces the night
The moon guards an ancient grave.

A ship ventures in the rough
The lighthouse speaks and guides the way,
Shadow mountains watch the show
Seabirds wait for another day.

In the silence of the black
Constellations watch the sky,
Peaceful mist engulfs the air
Spirit clouds drifting by.

A KING'S DREAM

Soft winds stroke the fertile earth
as passing clouds sprinkle
the land with life's nourishment.

The radiating sky is sieged
by a passionate sun
as lustful rays reach out
to touch the heavens.

Shades of green smother the land
and visions of a king's dream
enlighten his mind.

Palm trees wave to the shore
watching the sands swallow
a continuous tide

THE WONDER OF DAY

Morning wakes, a glorious ray of light
To see blue skies with just a touch of clouds
The wonder of day, farewell mysterious night

Children play and cry in keen delight
Their distant voices, how happily they sound
Morning wakes, a glorious ray of light

Far off a child has wings, a homemade kite
As daffodils watch together in a crowd
The wonder of day, farewell mysterious night

The sun stares, piercing and so bright
Guarding from high, shining strong and proud
Morning wakes, a glorious ray of light

A boy and his dog run where the grass is high
A farmer's field which soon will feel the plow
The wonder of day, farewell mysterious night

The sun in its chariot is now in total flight
Apollo guiding the reins will make us bow
Morning wakes, a glorious ray of light
The wonder of day, farewell mysterious night

DISCOVERY

Upon the rocking vessel he stands
Gazing towards the luscious land
With shades of black, green, and gold
A piece of earth to smell and hold

Beneath the clouds the island grows
From the peaks the water flows
A feasting land in isolation
Found by a sailor's imagination

A rugged coast with daunting cliffs
Beyond the shores the current drifts
Beaten beaches smoothed by tides
A secret cove where treasure hides

Hidden below the grainy crust
Magma flows, soon to thrust
Fertile richness feeding roots
Jungle canopy bears its fruits

Mesmerized by the virgin land
Discovery by a restless man
Surrounded by an expansive sky
A place to live, a place to die

THE CANYON

Following the river's edge
Rapids roar through the canyon
A quiet pool awaits the strong
As secrets lay beneath the surface

Jagged rocks smoothed by time
Heated by the dazzling sun
Struggling waves shaping sand
Watching footprints fade away

Gentle winds temper the earth
Challenging cliffs cast a shadow
Weakened trees sickly dying
Understand the fate of life

Whispers shouting from the waters
Careless moments captivate
Intense endurance is the flavor
Not for the meek and foolish

Underneath a torrid current
Liquid power detonates
Rushing towards the open basin
Strengthened bravo rule the land

WAKING UP

The radio opened up my eyes
A 70s ballad in my ear
Reaching over I stopped the noise
Silence was what I wanted to hear.
I laid resting on the bed
Waiting for another song
My lazy body began to stir
As I tried to move along.
I told her to wake-up first
She told me to go ahead
I was thinking of last night
Hoping to drag myself from bed.
The morning news caught my ear
A pillow wedged between my legs
What is there to eat today?
Yogurt, watermelon, maybe eggs
I shuffled to the bathroom sink
Splashing water on my face
Lathered up and shaven nubs
Then I let her have her space.
Brewed the coffee, packed the lunch
Picked-up the towel from the floor
Making certain the closet was closed
As we rushed outside the door.

OUR CHILDREN GROW

Our children grow before our eyes
The path of life in their control
A living link into the stars
The cycle makes the moment whole

A rising sun, a goddess moon
Currents circling a delicate globe
Hardened like a frozen pond
Softness like a velvet robe

Our children grow before our eyes
Changing seasons moving forth
Common passions that we share
Going south, east, west, and north

Perils as we wake each day
Stumbling on the lengthy trail
Climbing towards the mountain top
Little time to think or fail

Our children grow before our eyes
To march across the wicked earth
Absorbing with their open minds
Beginning from a painful birth

A destiny within their hands
In our dreams they do seek more
Our children grow before our eyes
In time of peace, In time of war

JAZZ NIGHT

Dressed up in my father's suit
Hear her play the silver flute,
Cuff links guard my clapping hands
As we listen to the bands,
Pocket watch will tick along
Feel the vibes of the upbeat song,
Tapping shoes with a polished shine
Patrons revel as they dine,
Golden clip secures my tie
Trumpet plays the notes so high,
Crisp and sharp my fitted cap
Silk and lace her stylish straps,
Music fills the void at night
Under stars melodic blight,
Happy movement on the floor
No one heading for the door,
Rhythm and chatter fill the room
Blaring horns, an evening boom,
Muscles move and bodies sweat
Swinging and dancing with no regret,
Busting a move for all to see
Enduring music, a legacy.

Surrounded by honesty

Engulfed in dignity

Smothered by integrity

Respect will be yours

*****

If you feel

a heart of steel

soon the lust

will start to rust.

If the heart

is made of stone

heaviness

may soon be known.

Sinking slowly

to the deep

what we allow

is what we reap.

FOREVER

Forever is farther than distant stars
More vast than an empty sky,
Forever compels poets to write
A lover to sing to a heart's delight.

Forever is an unknown journey
A visionary path which has no end,
Forever evokes youthful dreaming
Full of hope and distinctive meaning.

Forever can be consequential
Leaving thinkers scholarly,
Forever makes a yearning mind
Passioned reason, a stirring find.

Forever is an infinite time
Lost restrictions fluttering in space,
Forever entails eternity
A mother's love always meant to be.

FULFILL MY DREAMS

Fulfill my dreams of endless love
Stoke the embers in my heart,
Grasp my spirit, hold it close
Whisper we will never part.

Engulf my body with your scent
Feel our auras warmly embrace,
Understand my every need
Memorize my yearning face

Grant my desire and wish for calm
Stormy minds must fade away,
Caress my body with your love
Euphoric feelings as we lay.

Surround my soul with lasting hope
Convince my mind you're always here,
Promise you will never leave
Dream with me, erase the fear.

ANTICIPATION

The rhythm of our bodies
moves like a classical symphony,
With precise and sound perfection
Fill the mind with adoration.

Your warm and caring smile
Radiates like stars on a moonless night,
Senses heighten with expectations
In this state of high elation.

Our emotions swell like the ocean
Filling needed desires,
Human urges in syncopation
Experience joy of anticipation.

WE ARE

We are two beings
With two lives
Moving like the ocean,
We are two hearts
With two minds
Constantly in motion.
Brought together
By our love
Needing one another,
We are two people
With two hearts
Together we are better.
We are two raindrops
On our journeys
Drifting to the earth,
We are two lives
With a beginning
Sharing a rebirth.

YOUNG LOVE

I yearn to see you every day
Caress you every night,
I yearn to hold you close to me
And make it feel so right.

When I see your caring eyes
And kiss your loving face,
There's nothing much more wonderful
Than feeling your embrace.

A magic surrounds the two of us
A force so real and strong,
Within your touch, within your breath
Is where I do belong.

I think about our happiness
A blessing from above
Is this the feeling that we share?
The magical gift of love.

I only know that here with you
Is where I want to be
Caring for and loving you
Always, endlessly.

LOST

Infiltrate a tortured heart
Cleanse my ailing wound,
Heal my broken injured soul
As I am marooned.

Stuck within a moment lost
With nowhere to turn,
Helpless with my sorrow's hurt
Feel a sizzling burn

Navigate the empty road
Try to cross the line,
Peer into the consciousness
Tell me what you find.

Integrate false happiness
Blinded by the love,
Soar beneath the cooling sun
Shadowing above

Feel a sudden rainstorm burst
Piercing from the sky,
Seep into the crevices
As the lone dove does cry.

Tanka

A Japanese poem consisting of five lines, the first and third with five syllables and the other lines with seven syllables. The thirty-one syllables create an image or expresses a mood. A form of waka or Japanese song and verse, tanka translates as 'short song.'

Covered by the sun
Vast empty island beaches
Waiting for footprints
Feel the touch of the ocean
Feel the breath of a light breeze

Thick bamboo forest
Blocks penetrating night light
In the black of the sky
A blanket of misty fog
Settles in the mountain pass

Whispering seashells
Waiting for the next high tide
Decorate the sand
Children with plastic buckets
Collect the ocean's bounty

Rounded Images
Of floating colors above
Arch across the lake
Fading double rainbow mist
Like water-colored paintings

As the sun slowly

Drops behind distant mountains

Cool air fills the sky

Warmth of the day disappears

Dew covers the fallen leaves

Constant wave movement

Rushing submerged lava flows

As fisherman wait

Patiently under the sun

Quietly beneath the moon

Scented homemade leis
Sweet plumeria flowers
Fragrance from the land
Adorning dancing keiki
At the annual May Day

As the crescent moon
Drifts high in the western sky
City lights sparkle
Rays from a contagious sun
Bounce on the lunar surface

Cold rain of winter
Filling barren dry streambeds
Soaking thirsty roots
As broken fallen tree limbs
Lay next to a travelled path

Petrified moments
A collage of memories
Lasting impressions
Never to be forgotten
Like a book of history

Quiet thoughts of calm
Serene peacefulness
Soothing a spirited soul
Laying under the willow
Resting with a gentle wind

Daydreams lively thoughts
Vivid imagination
Exploring my mind
While I sleep under the stars
Inspirational visions

Snow covered mountains

Border empty open skies

Waiting for a storm

To drop more crystal raindrops

Creating winter's presence

River of white foam

Bolting toward open spaces

Summer approaches

Steeply cascading waterfall

Thunderous descent below

Precious are moments

Gathered from many seasons

From new life to death

Filled with smiles and happiness

Somewhere beneath a rainbow

Life's epiphany

Searching for a creator

Reason for being

True wisdom with compassion

Embedded awakening

Haiku

A Japanese poem of seventeen syllables in three lines of five, seven, and five. Traditionally, haiku evokes images of nature or the seasons. Non-traditional haiku have also evolved and become commonplace.

Beautiful Hula

Graceful dancers in the spring

Like floral blossoms

Capture summer's wind

Place it deep within your heart

Share the warmth of love

A fatal rainbow

Reaching across the valley

Quietly disappears

Cold relentless waves
Batter the lonesome buoy
Tired seabirds rest

Peacefulness abounds
The unwinding of summer
As soothing clouds smile

From a mother's heart
Pure unconditional love
Family blessing

Lasting commitment
True inspirational love
Two hearts become one

Majestic summit
Rising to Heaven's altar
As spring is reborn

A spring day ends
As the vanishing sun fades
Night sky awakens

A shattered nightmare

Caught beyond my inner self

Defeated by hope

Reflections of life

A mending broken heart

Uncover hidden truths

Travel a worn path

To a place beyond your mind

Where dreams do come true

Eternity lives

Where spirits seek lasting peace

Deep beyond the light

Search beyond your dreams

Lead your heart to happiness

Where love can be found

To gaze in the night

Dazzled by one million stars

Divine creation

Filtered rays of sun
Pierce the cool fertile forest
As morning begins

Early autumn snow
Soft velvet blanket of rain
Fallen frozen mist

Rushing waters flow
Surge over ancient boulders
To Pacific shores

Open ocean swells

Greeting a hardened coastline

As Winter waves roll

The lonely highway

Calling my name as I sleep

Tempting lasting dreams

Icy rain and flakes

Adorning the wilderness

December snowstorms

Stoke recurring dreams
Challenge your abilities
Success awaits you

Find within your heart
Home for trust and loyalty
Where love will blossom

The falling sunshine
Fire in a distant sky
Igniting darkness

Seek the resting sun

For beyond the horizon

A new day begins

Embrace destiny

The travelled path of your dreams

A journey with hope

Summer's crashing waves

Fluid touch of artistry

Pleasant kiss of mist

A quiet moment
On peaceful tranquil waters
Soothing mind and soul

Glorious sunset
As fractured clouds fill the sky
Waiting for the night

Under a vast sky
Gathering clouds hide the sun
Playful summer day

Sliver in the sky

Surrounded by sparkling stars

July crescent moon

Enduring hardships

Like ice from a winter freeze

Melt with a warm hug

To love is to live

The joyfulness of your heart

Begins with a smile

Tapestry of life
Woven with the threads of time
Spun from birth to death

Landed cardinal
Upon a skinny bare branch
Swaying with the wind

Sweet ripened mango
Hanging from the aged tree
Feast for hungry birds

RAIN...

Gentle raindrops

fall upon my head.

Without my hat

they trickle

down my face.

Like teardrops,

they trickle

down my chin.

Soon,

liquid bombs strike me.

Rain stains my shirt

streaming down

my sticky back.

Tiny puddles

cover my glasses,

as fresh showers

hurry walkers.

Sun rays break

the peppered clouds

as the soft wet

drizzle fades.

Tender rain caresses

the thirsty plants,

while a windy sun

dries my head.

Song Lyrics: PARADISE IS MY HOME

These are my islands

At the end of my rainbow

This is my paradise

This is my home

Where the sea is clear and blue

Where the sunshine is golden

This is where I belong

Paradise is my home

The people are friendly and warm

Like the land around me

And flowers bloom everywhere

Full of beauty and scented smells

The locals work all day long

And at night they sing their songs

This is where I belong

Paradise is my home

Where the sea is clear and blue

The sunshine is golden

This is where I belong

Paradise is my home.

Song Lyrics: ISLANDS OF LOVE

Amidst the blue Pacific

Where the sun was born

The nights are clear and breezy

Just like the early morn

Love is deep and giving

Love is long and true

I'll see you at these islands

Amidst the ocean blue.

We'll walk within the valleys

We'll walk beneath the trees

The wind will call our names at night

We'll hear it in the breeze

Our love will grow so much each day

The love we share so new

I'll see you in our islands

Amidst the ocean blue.

Hawai'i... Where we shall meet

Hawai'i... I will kiss so sweet

Hawai'i... The islands, the islands of love.

NEVER AGAIN, NEVER FORGET

*This poem is dedicated to the Japanese Americans forced into
internment camps during WWII. I wrote this poem after I visited the
Honouliuli internment camp in Central Oahu.*

I see the image of his face
As we remember this infamous place,
Birds are singing in the trees
A calming stream flows to the sea,
People once taken from their homes
On a journey to the unknown,
Families saddened and torn apart
Kept together by loving hearts,
Men of stature and dignity
Consumed by a frenzied inequity,
Who knows where their souls have gone
But the memory lingers on,
Amidst the pain and tears we shed
We honor the living, we honor the dead,
Reasoned thinking gone astray
Lost, but found on another day,
Fathers, wives, children, men
Shall not be imprisoned, never again,
A nation's deed, remorseful regret
A moment in time we'll never forget

ANTI-WAR : WAR NO MORE

EMPTY BOOTS

Sadness ascended upon the air
Another coffin from the plane
Families filled with grief and despair
Feeling their loss, experiencing pain.

How many more will return with our flag?
Empty boots a symbol of death
How many will sleep in a body bag?
Soldiers who gasp their final breath.

When will it end? this conflict, this war
So much effort for a controversial cause
Americans asking: What is it for?
Questionable decisions and leadership flaws

We went looking for WMDs
Weapons owned by an evil man
Ignoring voices of opposing pleas
Our soldiers invaded a foreign land

Many more heroes and civilians will die
Loved ones will worry and shed their tears
Mothers and fathers and children will cry
Little may change for many years

We want them home, we want them back
Brave fighting soldiers doing their part
From Afghanistan to the depths of Iraq
Heroes with courage, sacrifice and heart

The wind has shifted and changed its course
Concrete attitudes must follow suit
Policy makers must show some remorse
Time to stop the empty boots.

WAR

War brings triumph
Heroes are born,
War has losses
Nations mourn,
War is a place
We don't want to be,
Let there be peace
In a world that is free.

FALLEN

You are fallen

But you stand tall.

You are gone

But within our hearts.

You are mourned

But you are reborn.

You are missed

And you are loved.

NORMALCY

Troops die on battlefields
Football players take the field

Explosions from roadside mines
College students sharpen their minds

Terrorists plan their next attack
Doctors heal a heart attack

Widows cry their tears at night
Restaurants open late at night

Refugees leave abandoned homes
Developers build single-family homes

Car bombs kill near crowded stores
Fashion jeans sold in Waikiki stores

Soldiers cautiously patrol the streets
A game of stick ball on the street

Anxious families afraid each day
Reporters tell the news each day

Snipers end another life
Lifeguards save one more life

The sun rises in the east
The sun sets in the west

IRAQ

The road is silent
The wind speaks
Sunlight shines
But the village sleeps,
Only the dust
Moves with the breeze.

A timid dog
Cowers in the shade
A convoy of armor
Rushes through the streets.

A bomb explodes
Three soldiers die
Another day in Iraq

DOMESTIC VIOLENCE

I heard a voice beyond the light
Someone talking, a stranger's plight
I was at peace, there was no fright
The moment was beginning

The voice broke the silent dark
In my soul, a quiet spark
Hollow thoughts, barren and stark
Kept the moment spinning

Between the sheets the echo came
The wilderness no longer tame
An angry voice was to blame
A moment far from winning

A single slap the silent broke
A heated rage, a fire stoked
Fright suddenly evoked
Unbridled untamed passion

BEYOND THE NIGHTMARE

Beyond the nightmare
There was a clearing
As strangers
Looked into a hole

A tired woman
Watched intently
And demons stared
From behind the knoll

A perished dream
About to vanish
With trifling thoughts
Shunned from the mind

The hungry earth
Absorbs the vanquished
To realize
An empty find

A broken stone
Rests by the fissure
Where the night dream
Disappears

A quiet scream
Is heard by no one
A moment becomes
Endless years.

I witnessed history in my sleep
A truck crashed into a rusted jeep
It happened in the month of May
When we were at the park to play
Screeching tires stained the road
Upon the sidewalk, a shifted load
Broken metal, shattered glass
Someone driving just too fast
A fire started at the scene
Bewildered was the startled teen
Flames and smoke were in the air
People watched, they stood and stared
A body laid upon the ground
Motionless without a sound
When I went to see his face
I woke up in another place

MISSING YOU

I miss your scent

I miss your taste

So many years

Did pass in haste

I miss your touch

Your gentle stroke

The loving words

That you once spoke

You're warm embrace

I'll never forget

My fractured path

I do regret

A magical moment

A broken soul

I will repair

The heart you stole.

Curiosity

Serendipity

Anonymity

In the city

Condo kitty

Tenants witty

Hope and pity

In the city

*****

Incarceration

Prison nation

Behind bars

Simplification

Not worth eating

Mental beating

Behind bars

Freedom fleeting

A DAY IN AMERICA

Too many guns
Another shooter
Too much crime
Another looter

Opulent riches
Homeless are many
Begging in the streets
For a dollar or pennies

A leader who lies
And sows division
No sense of remorse
No act of contrition

High technology
Low self-esteem
Mental illness
A lost young dream

Families struggle
Increasing costs
Within our schools
Innocence lost

Hope and compassion
People who care
Helping the needy
In their despair

Questionable policing
Anger and hate
Time for compassion
De-escalate

Moments of happiness
Finding the glory
Warriors of change
Rewriting the story.

The person looked beyond a dream
A life had lost its bursting steam
Attempts were made to gain control
From falling in the deepening hole.
The rainbow lingered in the air
A brilliant show without compare
Symbolic of possibilities
Inspiring life's tranquilities
For moments fleeting come and go
Insisting on the next great show
Challenges to conquer fear
Celebrations with those so dear
A time to grasp the golden ring
To hear the glorious angels sing
For in the end the sun will shine
And brighten lives 'til the end of time.

BE

Be humble, don't be vain

Be forgiving, don't be angry

Be assertive, don't be aggressive

Be accepting, don't be envious

Be genuine, don't be fake

Be understanding, don't be annoyed

Be active, don't be complacent

Be prepared, don't be surprised

Be engaged, don't be silent

Be involved, don't be indifferent

Be smart, don't be careless

Be respectful, don't be rude

Be compassionate, don't be uncaring

Be patient, don't be rushed

Be kind, don't be mean

Be an advocate

Be a voice

Be a friend

Haiku

Brown chameleon

Darts through the leafy ficus

Slowly becomes green

Red hibiscus

Royal hue of monarchs past

Soft velvet richness

Delicate blossoms

Beneath lush thick canopies

Waiting to be found

Full moon inspired

Reflecting on the ocean

Towards distant shores

Midnight star gazers

Skilled ocean navigators

Journey on the waves

Sailing on the sea

Masters of Hokulea

Explore foreign lands

Orange purple sky

Grazing on the horizon

A resting sun sleeps

Disappearing fog

Rolling from the open sea

Drifts with the brisk wind

Invisible smell

Adorning fragrance lingers

Candles light the way

Cotton candy clouds

Hiding winter's sky and sun

Snowstorms approaching

Yellow, pink, red shades

Plumeria tapestry

Surrounds the garden

Sturdy sunflowers

Following a solar trail

Stare at fleeting clouds

Swirling bamboo fan

Cooling the warm Ewa heat

As the trade winds rest

Summer rainbow fades

Towering palms brush the sky

A softy sprinkle falls

Sound of autumn rain

On rooftops and umbrellas

Mother earth nourished

On the Ewa Plain
Old plantation trees of shade
Refreshing relief

New blossoms of spring
Colorful and delicate
Mom's special garden

Young daring sparrow
Struggling against the spring breeze
Learning how to fly

Awake with the moon
Gratitude for life's blessings
To see a shooting star

Delicate orchid
Like a fragile masterpiece
Scented with beauty

Falling with a veil of mist
As the sun breaks through
Soft summer raindrops

Towering sea cliffs
Guardian of sacred land
Touched by summer clouds

Golden eastern sky
Silhouette of Diamond Head
A new day begins

Splendor of yellow
Glorious regal bouquet
Floral fireworks

A red gray flow

Creeps to abandoned houses

Pele reclaims her land

Fountains of lava

Spewing from the broken crust

Red glowing fire

The dance of Pele

Eruption of liquid rocks

Smoldering landscape

Oh, living mountain
Awake from your dormant sleep
Show your mighty strength

Creating new land
Pele shares ancient magic
Since the beginning

Last burst of sunlight
Filters onto mountain trails
Diminishing rays

My love for you grows

Cherishing time together

Today and all days

Like a moving stream

searching for the deep water

I seek my true love

A welcoming touch

Awakens sleeping senses

Gentle strokes of love

Her soft smooth body
Moves with anticipation
Desires are stirred

Find within your heart
Home for trust and honesty
Where love will blossom

My love for you lives
Feelings of lost memories
Quietly linger

Gusting city winds
Ladybug taking a break
Resting on my sleeve

Seven butterflies
Playing on a spring day
Like restless children

Graceful humpback whales
Swimming in the ocean deep
Disappear like ghosts

Silent manta ray
Flawlessly gliding
Above the tranquil sand

Four golden finches
Darting amongst stranded trees
Follow the leader

Two red dragonflies
Hover above the water
Like helicopters

Lone caterpillar

Nestled within nature's womb

Waiting for spring wings

Autumn equinox

Greets changing winds of summer

As warm breezes cool

A captured nightmare

Hidden beyond winter's storm

Infiltrates the mind

Vast stillness above
Looking to the summer moon
As crickets chatter

In turquoise waters
Calm swells quietly arrive
Stroking coastal shores

To love is to dream
A special place in the heart
Shared with your best friend

GOODBYE

Farewell, farewell my special friend
Your time on earth has come to an end
The suffering and pain no more
Now your spirit and soul do soar

Beyond the darkness, past the light
Your energy has taken flight
A journey to another place
Enactment of the final embrace

Creativity does abound
But with no words or any sound
A time to follow the weathered path
Harmonious without the wrath

Goodbye my friend, an era done
We captured the moon, conquered the sun
Experienced dreams and visions cast
Who knew the days would be our last

(Dedicated to Fred Vanderpoel)

REFLECTIONS OF MY DAD

I looked into the portal of his mind
A broken body weakly cried
The wit of genius was alive
Unspoken words described his soul

Careless sentences torched my being
Tired eyes with a yearning look
Words wanting older desires
Spoke loudly of another time

I saw a man once so emboldened
Holding on to precious life
Into the darkness, he would stare
Counting memories in the night

A lifetime filled with cherished dreams
Atop a mountain of treasured love
Beneath a pool of melting hope
Breaching pathways towards the sky

Other books by Will Espero

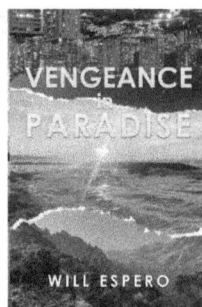

Other JMFdeA Press Books

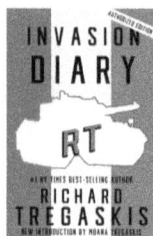